Date: 3/22/21

J BIO OBAMA
Nichols, Catherine,
Barack Obama : our 44th
president /

BARACK
OBAMA

OUR 44TH PRESIDENT

by Catherine Nichols

The Child's World®
childsworld.com

1980 Lookout Drive • Mankato, MN 56003-1705
800-599-READ • www.childsworld.com

ACKNOWLEDGMENTS
Content Adviser: David R. Smith, Adjunct Assistant Professor
of History, University of Michigan–Ann Arbor; Cary R. Covington,
Associate Professor of American Politics, University of Iowa

PHOTOS
Cover and page 3: Library of Congress, Prints and Photographs
Division (detail)
Interior: Associated Press, 22, 23, 25, 27, 33, 34, 35, 36, 39 (right);
Brian Cassella/MCT/Newscom, 31, 39 (left); Courtesy Barack Obama
Presidential Library, 11, 28, 29; Erik S. Lesser/ZUMA Press/Newscom,
24; JOHN GRESS/REUTERS/Newscom, 19, 38 (right); John Lee/
MCT/Newscom, 20; Joshua Lott/AFP via Getty Images, 37; Kyodo
via AP Images, 9; Marc Serota/Getty Images News via Getty Images,
30; OBAMA PRESS OFFICE/UPI/Newscom, 4, 5, 7, 12, 13, 15, 38
(left); PVDE/Bridgeman Images, 8; Steve Liss/The LIFE Images
Collection via Getty Images, 17; Topps/Splash News/Newscom, 16

ISBN 9781503844353 (REINFORCED LIBRARY BINDING)
ISBN 9781503846852 (PORTABLE DOCUMENT FORMAT)
ISBN 9781503848047 (ONLINE MULTI-USER EBOOK)
LCCN 2019957808

Printed in the United States of America

CONTENTS

Barack Obama served as president from 2009 to 2017.

A MULTICULTURAL CHILDHOOD

For many years, Barack Obama struggled to make sense of his **multicultural heritage.** He is the son and grandson of people who came from Kansas in the center of the United States. He is also the son and grandson of people who came from a small village in Kenya in East Africa. He grew up in Honolulu, Hawaii, and Jakarta, Indonesia.

Barack's mother, a young woman named Ann Dunham, had moved from Kansas to Hawaii with her family during her teen years. Barack's father, who was also named Barack Obama, had a different story. As a boy, he had tended goats in his father's village in Kenya. Obama Sr. did well in school, and he received a **scholarship** to study at the University of Hawaii. That's where the two young people met and fell in love. They married in 1960, and on August 4, 1961, their son was born.

Barack Obama was born in Hawaii. Here, he is pictured at his home in Honolulu around 1964.

When Barack was two years old, his father was offered a scholarship to study at Harvard University in Massachusetts. The scholarship would pay for school and his expenses, but included no money to support his family. Obama Sr. was ambitious. He felt he couldn't turn down such an offer. He left for Harvard, while Barack and his mother stayed behind in Hawaii. Barack would not see his father again for eight years.

Barack was close to his mother. She always made him feel special. She taught him to have **empathy** for other people. If he did or said something thoughtless or unkind, she'd ask, "How would that make you feel?" She also had a great sense of wonder—about people, paintings, poetry, music, and nature. When they walked together in the evening, she'd tell Barack to close his eyes and listen to the rustling leaves. Sometimes she'd wake him in the middle of the night to look at an especially bright and beautiful moon.

The name Honolulu comes from two words in Hawaiian: *hono*, "a joining together," and *lulu*, "a shelter from the wind." People from many backgrounds have joined together to make this city. Some have roots in China, Japan, and the Philippines. Others moved to Hawaii from the mainland United States.

Barack was also close to his grandparents, Madelyn and Stanley Dunham. He called his grandmother "Toot." His grandfather was "Gramps." Barack remembers going swimming and spearfishing with Gramps in the sparkling waters around Honolulu. Once they went to Hickam Air Force Base to watch astronauts return from space. Barack sat on his grandfather's shoulders to get a good view.

In 1964, Barack's mother filed for divorce from his father, and she soon married again. Her new husband, Lolo Soetoro, came from the country of Indonesia. He was in Hawaii as a student.

In 1965, some Indonesians rebelled against their government. The Indonesian government then required all Indonesian students studying abroad to return home. In 1967, six-year-old Barack moved with his mother and stepfather to Jakarta, the capital of Indonesia.

Indonesia was a poor country. Many people lived in mud and brick huts. They washed themselves and their clothing in the river. There were few cars in the country. Instead, many people rode bicycles that pulled small, two-wheeled carriages. Barack's family lived in a small house on the edge of the city. The house had no air-conditioning, no refrigerator, and no flushing toilet.

Barack's mother's full name was Stanley Ann Dunham. She was given the name Stanley by her father, who had hoped (before she was born) that she would be a boy. She went by her middle name, Ann.

***Barack* means "blessed" in Arabic.**

***Toot* is short for *tutu*, the Hawaiian word for "grandmother."**

Barack's mother and stepfather couldn't afford to send him to one of the special schools where most American children in Jakarta went. Instead, he went to the local school with Indonesian children. In first grade, Barack wrote an essay. It was called "I Want to Become President." Barry, as everybody called him, was full of dreams for the future even then.

Indonesia was a wonderful place for an adventurous young child. Barack had lots of new experiences and explored many new places. He remembers "days of chasing down chickens and running from water buffalo, nights of shadow puppets and ghost stories and street vendors bringing . . . sweets to our door." Alligators, ducks, and chickens lived in his yard.

Barack Obama (circled) attended a neighborhood school in Jakarta. Classes were taught in Indonesian, so his mother made him get up early to do extra homework in English.

Best of all was Tata, a gibbon that played in the trees overhead. His stepfather had brought the wild ape all the way from the island of New Guinea as a gift for Barack. Soetoro treated Barack like a son. Once Soetoro bought him boxing gloves and taught him how to defend himself.

Barack made friends among the Indonesian children, though sometimes his classmates could be cruel. He was the only student from another country and looked different than his classmates. Though they teased him at times, Barack's classmates were also curious. Barack liked to show them the book about Disneyland that his grandmother had sent him. They also liked to look through a catalog from the United States, admiring all the wonderful things there were to buy.

Barack's mother taught her son to be proud of his heritage as an African American. She told him about people like Martin Luther King Jr., one of the leaders of the effort to gain **civil rights** for all Americans. She also worried that her son wasn't getting the education he needed. She sent to the United States for teaching materials. She woke Barack up every morning at four o'clock and spent three hours teaching him. Barack grumbled sometimes. "This is no picnic for me either, buster," his mother said.

Finally, Barack's mother decided that he would get a better education in Hawaii. When he was 10, she took him back to Honolulu to live with his grandparents and attend Punahou (Poon-a-ho) School. It was an expensive private school with an excellent reputation. Most of the students were of European or Asian background and came from well-known and well-to-do families. Barack's grandparents worked hard to help send him there.

In Indonesia, Barack tasted many foods that were new to him, including snake and grasshopper. He has said that snake meat is tough and that roasted grasshoppers are crunchy.

Barack is pictured here on a school trip in 1972. He sometimes felt out of place at the Punahou School because many of the students came from wealthy families.

On his first day at his new school, Barack's teacher introduced him to the other students in his class. They laughed at his unusual name. When they found out that his father came from Kenya, they made jokes. From then on, the other kids weren't mean to him. They just ignored him. He was too different. He didn't even play the same games. He had learned to play soccer and badminton in Jakarta. He didn't know how to play football or ride a skateboard like the Hawaiian kids. Most days, Barack went right home after school to read comics or watch TV by himself.

At Christmas that year, he had a surprise visitor—his father, Barack Obama Sr. He came to Hawaii to see his son and to recover from a car accident. Barack barely remembered him. But he had heard about him. Barack's mother wanted her son to be proud of his father and his heritage. She told him that his father was an important leader in Kenya who worked to help people improve their lives. Barack also learned that he had half-brothers and a half-sister he had never met.

At first, father and son were uncomfortable with each other. Once, Barack's father ordered him to turn off the TV and study. Barack ran into his room and slammed the door. Barack's teacher invited his father to give a talk.

While she lived in Jakarta, Barack's mother worked teaching English to Indonesians.

Barack's father belonged to the Luo ethnic group in Kenya. It is the nation's third-largest ethnic group.

Barack was afraid the other students would tease him even more. Obama Sr. spoke of the wild animals that ran free in his country. He told of young boys who had to kill a lion to prove they were men. He told of Kenya's long years of struggle to be free. The class was impressed. One boy who had teased Barack said, "Your dad is pretty cool." At the end of the month, Obama Sr. returned to Kenya. Barack would never see him again.

Soon after, Barack's mother and stepfather separated. She returned to Honolulu with his half-sister, Maya. Barack moved into an apartment with them. A few years later, his mother returned to Indonesia to study **anthropology.** Barack chose to stay behind with Toot and Gramps.

CHAPTER TWO

DREAMS FROM HIS FATHER

Barack enjoyed his six years at Punahou School. The campus was beautiful. The other students were relaxed and easy to talk to once they got to know him. They called him Barry. He hung out with his many friends. He played on the school's championship basketball team, although he spent more time on the bench than he liked. He enjoyed reading and singing in the school choir.

But Barack's teen years were not perfect. For one thing, he missed his mother and Maya. He saw them only a few times a year. And he didn't always like following his grandfather's rules, such as filling the gas tank when he borrowed the car. He'd argue, listing reasons the rules weren't fair. Because he was good at arguing, he often left Gramps with nothing to say.

After awhile, Barack began to see things from his grandfather's point of view. He thought of the struggles Gramps had gone through and of his need to feel respected in his own home.

Barack Obama's yearbook picture from Punahou School in 1979

"I recognized," Barack wrote, "that sometimes he really did have a point, and that in insisting on my own way all the time, without regard to his feelings or needs, I was in some way **diminishing** myself." This was the empathy that Barack's mother had tried to teach him. Now he was beginning to understand it for himself. Empathy would become, Obama says, a "**guidepost** for my **politics**."

Under apartheid, the South African government put people into different racial categories. Black South Africans couldn't live in the same areas, hold the same jobs, or go to the same schools as white South Africans. Thanks to the efforts of leaders such as Nelson Mandela, South Africa's law of racial separation ended in February 1991.

Although Barack made friends at school, he sometimes felt like an outsider. Very few students there were African American. He became friendly with an older student who also had a multicultural background. The two young men had long talks. "Growing up," Obama has said, "I wasn't always sure who I was or what I was doing." He was trying to find out.

Barack graduated from high school in 1979. By this time, he had chosen to attend Occidental College, a small college in Los Angeles, California, because a girl he liked was enrolling there. At age 18, Barack went to live on the mainland United States for the first time in his life.

Barack did well at Occidental. He enjoyed himself and made new friends. He also got involved in politics for the first time. When students on campus held a rally against **apartheid,** a racist policy in South Africa, he was one of the speakers.

Occidental was a small college. After attending for two years, Barack was ready to stretch his wings and see more of the world. He applied and was accepted to Columbia University in New York City.

At Columbia, Barack majored in **political science.** He had become more serious about his studies. He turned down invitations to parties in order to stay home and study. The rest of the time he explored the city. He saw skyscrapers being built and streets full of people with plenty of money to spend in dazzling shops. He also saw abandoned buildings in poor neighborhoods, people sleeping on the sidewalk, and people selling drugs openly on the street.

Soon after Barack graduated in 1983, he received a telephone call from Kenya. His father had been killed in an automobile accident. Barack hardly knew how he should feel. He hadn't seen his father since that monthlong visit 10 years before. He had written letters and received some back, but the letters had grown fewer and fewer on both sides over the years. Still his father, his father's family, and his father's country were all somehow part of him. How could Barack know who he was if he didn't know them? He vowed that someday he would travel to Kenya and learn more about that part of himself.

COMMUNITY ORGANIZING

Community organizers help people in a community come together to solve their problems. They might work with renters' groups worried about large rent increases on their apartments, or bus riders unable to get to work because bus service has been cut back. They might help poor people organize to keep a neighborhood grocery store open.

Community organizers don't solve people's problems. Instead, they teach people how to solve problems for themselves. Organizers show people how to run meetings, how to be comfortable speaking in public, and how to reach agreements with **landlords,** employers, and politicians. Organizers knock on doors to meet the people in their community. They encourage people to vote and to come to meetings to discuss their problems and figure out how to solve them. They work to bring groups together to get to know each other and help each other out.

Community organizing isn't easy. The pay is low and the hours are long. Organizers have to be good at listening to what other people say. They have to remember that their job is to help others learn to lead, not to be leaders themselves. But many people find the job satisfying because they are helping improve people's lives. Barack Obama's early experience as a community organizer prepared him to work with diverse groups of people on the **campaign** trail and as president. The picture below shows Obama working as a community organizer in Chicago.

For now, however, he longed for a place to live in in the United States where he could put down roots and feel at home. He also wanted to find work to do that would be useful and help people. Obama decided to move to Chicago, Illinois, and become a community organizer. He would try to help poor people come together to help themselves.

After trying for six months, he finally got a job with the Developing Communities Project, a church-based community organization on Chicago's South Side. This was a run-down section of the city. Some people in the community were discouraged. Jobs had disappeared. Housing was badly in need of repair. Obama didn't earn much money at his job as a community organizer, but he didn't care. He discovered he was good at talking to people and getting them to trust him. He got people to work together to get what they needed.

Three years later, Obama was ready to move on. He was proud of what he'd accomplished, but he wanted to do more. "The victories were small," says a man he worked with. "They changed people's lives, but they didn't change American society and he wanted to do that."

At age 26, Obama was accepted to Harvard Law School in Cambridge, Massachusetts. It is one of the most respected law schools in the country. At Harvard, he could acquire the knowledge, friends, and power to bring about real change. A Harvard education, Obama has said, "means you can take risks. You can try to do things and still land on your feet."

During these years, Obama remained close to his family. His stepfather died in 1987. After that, his relationship with his half-sister, Maya, changed. He "really took on the role of a father," she says. He didn't forget his own father, either. Before entering law school, Obama finally made the journey to Kenya that he'd promised himself.

Obama met many relatives in Kenya—a step-grandmother, half-brothers, a half-sister, aunts, uncles, and cousins. He got to know these family members he had never met before. They took him on a journey to the home in the country where his grandparents had lived. When Obama saw his father's grave, he knelt and wept. He was sad, but he was at peace. With a stronger sense of who he was, he could get on with his life.

The *Harvard Law Review* is one of the most respected legal journals in the United States. Presidents of the review have gone on to become university presidents, governors, and Supreme Court justices.

After his first year in law school, Obama got a summer job as an **intern** at a Chicago law firm. A young woman named Michelle Robinson was his adviser. She had gone to law school right after college and was already working as a lawyer.

Barack and Michelle Obama (pictured in 2004 in Chicago) have two children, Malia (right) and Sasha.

Obama liked Michelle very much, and he began asking her out on dates. At first, Michelle refused. She felt it wasn't appropriate since she was his adviser. Eventually, she agreed. They began their relationship sitting on a curb eating ice cream cones. They continued their relationship after Obama went back to Harvard. In his second year of law school, Obama was elected president of the *Harvard Law Review*. He was the first African American to receive this honor.

After graduating from law school in 1991, Obama moved back to Chicago. He had come to feel at home in the city, and it was where Michelle was. He knew he wanted to marry her. He also knew they would both want to live close to her family.

Barack and Michelle married in October 1992 in Chicago. Their first child, Malia, was born in 1998. A few years later, in 2001, their second daughter, Natasha, was born. They call her Sasha for short. It seemed Obama was in Chicago to stay.

Malia's name has two meanings. In Hawaiian, it means "calm." In Swahili, an African language, it means "queen."

ENTERING POLITICS

While living in Chicago with his young family, Obama worked as a lawyer for several years. He also taught **constitutional** law at the University of Chicago for 12 years. "I loved the law school classroom," Obama says. He enjoyed teaching about the US **Constitution** because he believes it shapes American attitudes.

In 1996, Obama ran for the Illinois state senate. After talking it over with Michelle, he entered the race. He won the election. During his time in the state senate, Obama was able to accomplish many things. He helped expand health care for children and change the state's death penalty system. But he was not successful in everything he tried.

In 2000, he ran for a seat in the US House of Representatives against **Democratic** congressperson Bobby Rush. Rush was well-known and well-liked by the people he represented, while Obama was a new-comer. Obama could not overcome Rush's popularity and lost the primary election.

Illinois state senator Barack Obama listens during a session in the senate chambers in Springfield, Illinois, in 2002. During this time, Obama also worked as a professor at the University of Chicago Law School.

Despite his defeat, Obama didn't lose his interest in politics. In 2003, he decided to run for the US Senate. That same year, John Kerry, a senator from Massachusetts, was the Democratic **candidate** for president. Obama spoke at some of Kerry's campaign events and impressed the senator. Kerry called Obama and asked him to give the main speech at the 2004 Democratic National **Convention.** After he hung up, Obama told aide Mike Signator, "I guess this is pretty big." Signator nodded. "I guess you could say that." It was bigger news than Obama realized.

While campaigning, Obama had met Americans who had told him of their efforts to succeed despite setbacks and hardships. No matter how impossible their dreams, they dared to keep hoping. He also remembered a sermon given by the minister of his church, Jeremiah A. Wright Jr. In this sermon, Wright talked about the "**audacity** of hope." Obama made this idea the focus of his speech.

On July 27, 2004, Obama spoke at the Democratic National Convention. Many listeners liked what he had to say. He talked about what united Americans, not about what divided them. "There is not a black America and white America and Latino America and Asian America—there's the United States of America," he said. Some people were even saying he might be the next president of the United States.

In the 2004 senatorial race, Obama's Republican candidate dropped out close to Election Day. The Republican Party could not find another strong candidate to replace him. Obama won election to the Senate with 70 percent of the vote. It was the largest victory for a statewide race in Illinois history.

MICHELLE OBAMA

Michelle Robinson grew up on Chicago's South Side. Her mother was a homemaker and, later, a bank secretary. Michelle's father worked at a city water plant. He had a disease called multiple sclerosis. Although his condition grew worse over time, he continued to work and care for his family.

Michelle was an excellent student and a good basketball player. After high school, she went to Princeton University, and then, like Obama, she studied law at Harvard. Michelle graduated from law school in 1988 and began working as an attorney at a law firm. After she married, Michelle left the law

firm and took public service jobs in Chicago. Her last position was as a vice president at the University of Chicago Hospitals. In 2007, she cut back her hours to help with her husband's campaign.

Michelle Obama spoke on the first night of the 2008 Democratic National Convention (pictured below). She told the audience that she and her husband believed "that you work hard for what you want in life, that your word is your bond, and you do what you say you're going to do, that you treat people with dignity and respect, even if you don't know them, and even if you don't agree with them."

Barack and Michelle Obama wave to the crowd at the Democratic National Convention in 2004 after Barack gave his speech.

After the convention, Obama returned to Illinois. In November, he won his election to the US Senate. For two years, Obama was very busy. He **sponsored bills,** worked on **committees,** and traveled all over the world. Obama believed that government could help people make the best use of their rights and freedoms. He believed two issues were the most important: ending the war in Iraq and giving all Americans access to affordable health care. Though he could work on these issues as a senator, he believed he would have more power to make change as president.

In February 2007, Obama announced he was running for president in the 2008 election. "I know I haven't spent a lot of time learning the ways of Washington," he said. "But I've been there long enough to know that the ways of Washington must change." Change was the rallying cry of Obama's campaign to win the Democratic **nomination** for president.

His main rival in the **primaries** was Senator Hillary Rodham Clinton from New York. Clinton was well-known, both as a senator and as the wife of former president Bill Clinton. She said she had the experience needed to be president and Obama did not.

During the primaries, videos appeared of sermons delivered by Obama's pastor and friend, Jeremiah Wright. In them, Wright said angry things about the US government and race in America. Many white people worried that Obama might feel the same. To address the uncomfortable issue of race, Obama gave a speech entitled "A More Perfect Union." He told white Americans about the hardships and **prejudice** a black man like Wright had endured in his life. He told black Americans that many whites also had hard lives and didn't like being blamed for what other white people had done in the past. Obama's speech was praised for its honesty and directness.

Obama greets supporters during a presidential campaign rally on the campus of Georgia Tech in Atlanta, Georgia, in 2007. An estimated 20,000 people attended the event.

Presidential candidates Senator John McCain (left) and Senator Obama shake hands before the start of a presidential debate in October 2008.

The primaries were hard fought. Obama won in some states. Clinton won in others. By June 3, people in all the states had voted. It was clear Obama would be the Democratic candidate, made official two months later at the Democratic National Convention. Obama selected Senator Joseph Biden of Delaware to run for vice president.

After the primaries, the Democrats turned their attention to the general election. Many voters were concerned about the **economy** and the war in Iraq. The Republican presidential candidate, Arizona senator John McCain, and Obama debated who would be the best leader in these difficult times. McCain said Obama didn't understand the main issues and didn't have enough experience. Obama claimed McCain still supported policies that had failed.

In September, two months before the election, the nation's economy was in a **crisis.** Many banks and other large companies had made risky decisions in previous years. Now they were in danger of going out of business. People across the country were worried about their jobs and savings. Many voters blamed the bad news on the Republicans in power. The Democratic candidate looked better and better.

Obama filled his office in Washington with photographs of his heroes. They include US presidents Abraham Lincoln and John F. Kennedy, civil rights leader Martin Luther King Jr., South African president Nelson Mandela, and boxer Muhammad Ali.

CHAPTER FOUR

PRESIDENT OBAMA

On November 4, 2008, more people cast votes than in any other presidential election. When the votes were counted, history had been made. Obama was the first African American president of the United States. That night, Obama stood before a crowd of more than 200,000 people in Chicago and spoke of the historic moment, "If there is anyone out there who still doubts that America is a place where all things are possible . . . tonight is your answer."

Obama had many ups and downs during his first four years as president. When he was sworn into office on January 20, 2009, the US and global economies were in deep **recessions.** Helping the US economy was his first task. In January and February 2009, Obama worked with a divided and **partisan** Congress to create a bill that would get the economy moving again by increasing the money being spent. He signed the bill into law on February 17. The new law pumped money into the economy through government spending and lowering taxes.

Two giant car companies, General Motors and Chrysler, were failing. They employed close to 1 million people. In March 2009, Obama directed the government to take over the automakers. The government gave the companies loans and made changes to how they operated. Both companies got back on their feet.

One of Obama's biggest campaign promises was to make health care more affordable. During 2009 and the beginning of 2010, he worked with Congress to pass a health care bill. If the bill passed, more money would go to government health programs. It would also make insurance companies cover people who were already sick. Those in favor of the bill said it would make getting health insurance easier for Americans. They also said it would make insurance cost less.

The stimulus bill Obama signed into law in 2009 was called the American Recovery and Reinvestment Act. Some of the bill's $787 billion was spent on building roads, bridges, and airports.

However, many people did not like the bill. No Republican in the House of Representatives voted for it. They said it made the government too big and took power away from states. They believed the bill's requirement that every person in the country be insured was unconstitutional. Despite these objections, Congress passed the bill and Obama signed the Affordable Care Act into law on March 23, 2010.

Barack Obama takes the oath of office on January 20, 2009, at the US Capitol. Obama had just become the first African American to be elected president of the United States.

President Obama, Vice President Biden, and members of the national security team watch an update in the Situation Room of the White House on the mission against Osama bin Laden.

In the November 2010 elections, voters showed they were upset with Obama's policies, especially his health care law. Republicans gained 60 seats in the House of Representatives and six seats in the Senate. Obama was becoming a tested leader. He dealt with political crises in Europe, an earthquake in Japan, and problems in the Middle East. In May 2011, Obama announced that a team of **Navy SEALs** had killed the terrorist leader Osama bin Laden, who was the mastermind behind the September 11, 2001, terrorist attacks. The dramatic event showed Obama was willing to take risks to protect the United States.

The economy was still the biggest issue facing the country when the 2012 presidential election season began. During much of 2011, three out of every four Americans thought the nation was headed in the wrong direction. In 2012, the unemployment rate remained above 8 percent. In the past, presidents have not been reelected when unemployment is that high. Yet more people said they approved of Obama's performance as president than those who said they didn't approve.

PARTISANSHIP: A DEEP DIVIDE

From the beginning of his presidency, Obama faced a lot of criticism for his policies. Many Republicans thought Obama was expanding the role of government more than he should. Many Democrats thought Obama wasn't doing enough, especially when it came to ending global warming and stopping the war in Afghanistan. Republican leaders in Congress often challenged the president. They tried to block his plans because they disagreed with the direction in which he wanted to take the country.

Obama came into office saying he wanted to shrink the partisan gap. But he found that goal difficult to achieve. In 2012, he told a television interviewer, "I haven't been able to change the atmosphere here in Washington to reflect the decency and common sense of ordinary people . . . who I think just want to see their leadership solve problems. And, you know, there's enough blame to go around for that."

Congress is organized along party lines. Democrats tend to support Democratic causes. Republicans lean toward Republican causes. Since the 1980s, the gap between the two parties has widened. A majority of members on both sides only want policies that support their beliefs. Partisanship makes it harder for the two sides to compromise. Without compromise, laws are difficult to pass. In the photo below, President Obama shakes hands with Republican Speaker of the House John Boehner before his address to Congress in 2011. The Republican Party gained control of the House of Representatives following the 2010 elections.

The day the Affordable Care Act was signed into law, 13 states sued to have it overturned. The lawsuit made its way to the US Supreme Court. In June 2012, the court ruled the health care law was constitutional and could proceed.

On May 5, 2012, Obama launched his campaign for reelection. He told supporters in Columbus, Ohio, "We have come too far to abandon the change we fought for these past few years. We have to move forward, to the future we imagined in 2008." The word *forward* became the slogan of his 2012 campaign.

Republicans chose Mitt Romney, a businessperson and former governor of Massachusetts, as their presidential candidate. Romney selected Paul Ryan as his vice presidential candidate. Ryan was a member of the US House of Representatives from Wisconsin. The Romney campaign blamed Obama for the poor economy and the high unemployment rate. The two Republicans promised voters that they would get the country back on track with spending cuts and tax breaks.

President Obama and Republican presidential candidate Mitt Romney (left) discuss the nation's issues during their final debate before Election Day.

In turn, Obama argued that no matter how bad the economy, a Romney administration would only make things worse. Obama said Romney's tax proposal would cut taxes for the wealthiest Americans and raise taxes on the middle class.

Going into the summer, polls showed the candidates in an even race. At the Democratic National Convention in September, Obama spoke about why he should be reelected. "I never said this journey would be easy," said the president, "and I won't promise that now. Yes, our path is harder, but it leads to a better place. Yes, our road is longer, but we travel it together."

The convention raised the president's popularity. By mid-September, 50 percent of registered voters favored Obama to be president. Forty-four percent favored Romney. Those numbers shifted during the final weeks of the race as undecided voters tried to make up their minds. Many questioned if they should give their current president four more years to get the economy moving again or they should trust that job to someone new.

Between the 2008 election and the 2009 inauguration, Obama wrote a children's book, *Of Thee I Sing: A Letter to My Daughters*. The book highlights 13 famous Americans whose traits he sees in his daughters, Malia and Sasha. The book was published in 2010.

The race went down to the wire. On November 6, 2012, more than 60 million voters officially voiced their opinions. They chose to give Obama another chance as president. Obama won a second term in the White House.

He spoke to a crowd of joyful supporters in Chicago, saying: "Tonight, in this election . . . the American people reminded us that while our road has been hard, while our journey has been long, we have picked ourselves up . . . and we know in our hearts that for the United States of America the best is yet to come."

Over the next four years, President Obama worked hard to fulfill his promises to the American people. He would face many challenges in his second term, starting with a mass shooting at Sandy Hook School in Newtown, Connecticut, in December 2012 that rocked the country to its core. Obama quickly called on Congress to enact gun-control legislation. He wanted to ban the sales of some powerful weapons and bring more attention to mental illness. However, the bill did not receive enough support in the Senate. When the bill was officially withdrawn, the president said it was "a pretty shameful day for Washington."

It seemed clear that Obama's second term was going to be a challenge. In 2013, arguments in the House and Senate over the federal budget caused a partial government shutdown for the first time in 17 years.

Government offices were closed, and hundreds of thousands of employees couldn't go to work. After more than two weeks, an agreement was reached, and Washington began to function again.

In the last years of his presidency, Obama began to use his power of executive action to handle issues that Congress couldn't—or wouldn't—address. He raised the hourly minimum wage for federal contract workers, and he directed the Environmental Protection Agency to create new rules for power plants. He used executive orders to reform US immigration policy, easing the way for children of illegal immigrants and granting work permits and legal status to more than 4 million immigrants who had entered the country illegally. He also became the first sitting US president to visit Cuba, improving US–Cuban relations that had been strained since the 1960s.

An executive order is the president's power to either make a new law or to enforce an existing one. Neither Congress nor the American people may approve executive orders— once the president issues an executive order, it is official and must be enforced.

President Obama meets with young undocumented immigrants in the Oval Office to discuss the impact of immigration policy on their lives. Obama's legislation focused on educational and employment opportunities rather than deportation.

Still, Republican politicians and voters weren't always happy with the job Obama was doing in his second term. During the midterm elections of November 2014, Republicans gained 12 seats in the House and retook control of the Senate. At the same time, a rash of race-related violent incidents plagued the country, shining a light on racial tension and police accountability across the United States. In 2015, Obama eulogized a shooting victim who was killed in a hate crime against a historically black church in Charleston, South Carolina. He said, "Perhaps this tragedy causes . . . us to examine what we're doing to cause some of our children to hate. Perhaps it softens hearts towards those lost young men . . . caught up in the criminal justice system and leads us to make sure that that system is not infected with bias; that we embrace changes in how we train and equip our police so that the bonds of trust between law enforcement and the communities they serve make us all safer and more secure."

The president and First Lady arrive at the White House after attending the memorial for one of the shooting victims at a historic black church in Charleston, South Carolina.

The White House was illuminated in rainbow colors to mark the US Supreme Court's ruling to legalize same-sex marriage. President Obama praised the Court's decision, saying, "All people should be treated equally, regardless of who they are or who they love."

While President Obama pushed back against renewed racial violence, he saw some progress on human rights in the courts. The Supreme Court ruled that state bans on same-sex marriage were unconstitutional. This ruling made same-sex marriage legal in the United States. The same week, the Supreme Court upheld Obama's health care plan, now commonly referred to as "Obamacare."

With a climbing approval rating during his final two years in office, President Obama focused on the issues that mattered to him the most, including gun control, climate-change regulations, and health care for all. When Obama delivered his final State of the Union speech, a seat was left empty in the gallery next to Michelle Obama, symbolizing the loss of life caused by gun violence. In the final weeks of his presidency, Obama campaigned for Hillary Clinton, the Democratic nominee. The Republican opponent, Donald Trump, vowed to undo many of Obama's policy achievements. In the end, Trump won the 2016 election and was set to become Obama's successor in the Oval Office.

At the end of his term, Obama and his wife purchased a home in Washington, DC, so that their younger daughter, Sasha, could finish out her high school years in the District. Since leaving office, both Michelle and Barack have remained busy, often making public appearances and holding speaking engagements. In 2018, Michelle released a memoir, *Becoming*, which sold over 1 million copies in its first week. Readers have gone on to purchase more than 10 million copies.

The Obamas have also remained active in the Obama Foundation, a Chicago-based nonprofit founded in 2014. The foundation's goals are to create the Barack Obama Presidential Center, support young leaders, and run the My Brother's Keeper Alliance, an organization supporting boys and young men of color. In 2018, Obama received the Robert F. Kennedy Human Rights' Ripple of Hope Award, celebrating leaders who are committed to social change. In 2019, he announced Redistricting U, an advocacy campaign that will fight against **gerrymandering.**

Out of the spotlight, the former president enjoys the chance to travel, rest, and relax after eight challenging years in the White House. He has made time for solo trips and family travel, including a family trip to Indonesia, where he lived for a portion of his childhood.

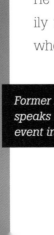

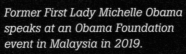

Former First Lady Michelle Obama speaks at an Obama Foundation event in Malaysia in 2019.

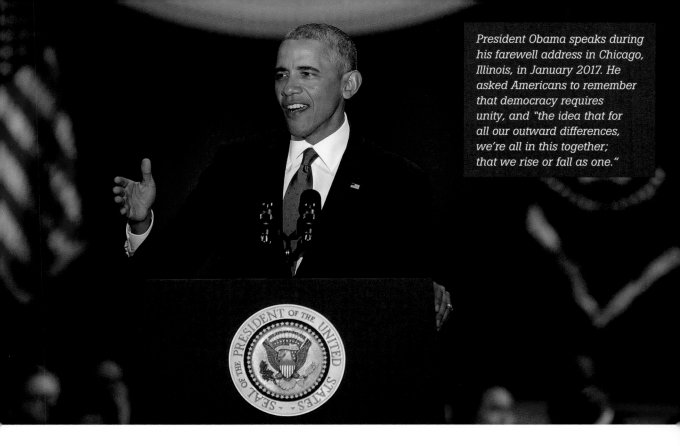

President Obama speaks during his farewell address in Chicago, Illinois, in January 2017. He asked Americans to remember that democracy requires unity, and "the idea that for all our outward differences, we're all in this together; that we rise or fall as one."

In his farewell address in January 2017, Barack Obama smiled amid the chants of "Four more years!" reminding the crowd that he was now a citizen, just like them. He then presented the American people with a parting challenge: "I'm asking you to believe. Not in my ability to bring about change—but in yours. I am asking you to hold fast to that faith written into our founding documents; that idea whispered by slaves and abolitionists; that spirit sung by immigrants and homesteaders and those who marched for justice; that creed reaffirmed by those who planted flags from foreign battlefields to the surface of the moon; a creed at the core of every American whose story is not yet written: Yes, we can."

Obama was awarded the Nobel Peace Prize in October 2009. The Nobel Committee honored the president for his "extraordinary efforts to strengthen international diplomacy and cooperation between peoples."

TIME LINE

1961
On August 4, Barack Hussein Obama is born in Honolulu, Hawaii. He is the son of Stanley Ann Dunham from Kansas and Barack Obama from Kenya.

1963
Barack Obama Sr. enrolls in Harvard University in Massachusetts, leaving his wife and son in Hawaii.

1967
Now divorced,

1971
Obama returns to Hawaii to live with his grandparents and attend Punahou School. His father comes from Kenya for a visit and stays a month.

1979
Obama enters Occidental College in California.

1981
Obama transfers to Columbia University in New York City, where he majors in political science.

1983
Obama graduates from Columbia University.

1985
Obama begins working as a community organizer in Chicago, Illinois.

1988
Obama makes a month-long trip to Kenya to visit his relatives. When he returns, he enters Harvard Law School.

1990
Obama is elected president of the *Harvard Law Review*, becoming the first African American to receive this honor.

1991
Obama graduates from law school and returns to Chicago. He becomes a professor of constitutional law at the University of Chicago.

1992
Obama marries attorney Michelle

2000
In February, Obama campaigns for a seat in Congress but loses in the Democratic primary to Bobby Rush.

2004
On July 27, Obama delivers the main speech at the Democratic National Convention. On November 2, he is elected a US senator.

2007
Obama announces he will run for president and begins his primary campaign.

2008
Obama defeats Senator Hillary Rodham Clinton of New York to become the Democratic presidential candidate. On November 4, Obama defeats Republican John McCain in the presidential election and becomes the first African American elected president of the United States.

2009
Obama is sworn in as president on January 20. Obama signs the American Recovery and Reinvestment Act into law on February 17. The law pumps $787 billion into the struggling US economy. In March, Obama directs the government to take over two failing carmakers, General Motors and Chrysler. In October, President Obama is awarded the Nobel Peace Prize.

2010
Obama signs the Affordable Care Act into law on March 23. In November, Republicans gain control of the House of Representatives. They also win six Senate seats.

2011
In May, Obama announces that terrorist leader Osama bin Laden has been killed by a team of Navy SEALs.

2012
Obama launches his campaign for reelection on May 5. Obama wins the presidential election on November 6. A mass shooting at Sandy Hook School in Newtown, Connecticut, prompts Obama to pursue stronger gun control laws.

2013
Partisan disagreements over the federal budget result in a 17-day partial government shutdown.

2015
Following a Supreme Court ruling, same-sex marriage is legalzed in all 50 states.

2018
Michelle Obama releases her bestselling memoir, *Becoming*. Her husband continues to work on his own memoir.

2019
Obama announces Redistricting U, an advocacy campaign fighting against gerrymandering.

anthropology (an-thruh-PA-luh-jee): Anthropology is the study of human societies and cultures. Obama's mother studied anthropology.

apartheid (uh-PAR-tyd): Apartheid was a system of legal racial discrimination in South Africa. Obama spoke out against apartheid while he was a college student.

audacity (aw-DA-suh-tee): Audacity is boldness or daring. Obama gave a speech on the audacity of hope.

bills (BILZ): Bills are ideas for new laws. A bill becomes law after both houses of Congress pass the bill and the president signs it.

campaign (kam-PAYN): A campaign is a group of activities designed to achieve a result. In 2007, Obama announced his campaign for the presidency.

candidate (KAN-duh-dayt): A candidate is a person who is running in an election. At least two candidates run for president every four years.

civil rights (SIV-ul RITES): Civil rights are the rights guaranteed by the Constitution to all citizens of the United States. Martin Luther King Jr. worked for the civil rights of African Americans.

committees (ku-MI-teez): Committees are groups of people who work on a particular problem or issue. Obama worked on many committees in the US Senate.

compromise (KOM-pruh-myz): Two people compromise when they each give up part of what they want in order to reach an agreement. As president, Obama tried to compromise with the US Congress.

Constitution (kon-stih-TOO-shun): A constitution is a set of basic principles that govern a society. The US Constitution promises certain rights to US citizens.

constitutional (kahn-stih-TOO-shunul): Something that is constitutional is related to the Constitution. Obama taught constitutional law at the University of Chicago.

convention (kun-VEN-shun): A convention is a meeting. The political parties each hold a national convention every four years to choose a presidential candidate.

crisis (KRYE-sis): A crisis is a difficult situation that needs immediate attention. In 2008, many people thought the US economy was in a crisis.

Democratic (dem-uh-KRAT-ik): If something is Democratic, it is related to the Democratic Party. Obama gave the main speech at the 2004 Democratic National Convention.

diminishing (duh-MIHN-ish-ing): If you are diminishing something, you are lessening its dignity or reputation. Obama felt that if he did not think about his grandfather's feelings, he was diminishing himself.

economy (ee-KA-nuh-mee): The economy is the way money is earned and spent in a country or area. During the 2008 campaign, many Americans were worried about the economy.

empathy (EM-pu-thee): Empathy is being aware of someone else's feelings and experiences. Obama's mother taught him the importance of empathy.

ethnic group (ETH-nik GROOP): An ethnic group is a group of people with common traits and customs and a sense of shared identity. Obama's father belonged to the Luo ethnic group.

gerrymandering (JEH-ree-man-dr-uhng): Gerrymandering is when a political group tries to change the boundaries of a voting district in order to help their party or hurt another party in elections.

guidepost (GIDE-post): A guidepost is something that serves as a clue to a complicated issue. Obama considers empathy a guidepost to his politics.

heritage (HAER-i-tij): A person's heritage is the cultural traditions and other things of value that have been passed down through the generations. Obama has a multicultural heritage.

intern (IN-turn): An intern is a student who works at a job, often without pay, to gain experience. During law school, Obama spent a summer working as an intern at a Chicago law firm.

landlords (LAND-lordz): Landlords are people who own houses or apartments they rent to other people. Community organizers help renters deal with landlords.

mainland (MAYN-land): The mainland is the main part of a continent or country, not including any islands. Obama lived on the US mainland for the first time when he was 18.

multicultural (mul-tee-KUL-chuhr-ul): If something is multicultural, it is made up of diverse cultures or ethnic groups. Obama has a multicultural background.

multiple sclerosis (MUL-tuh-pul skluh-ROW-sis): Multiple sclerosis is a disease involving the brain and spinal cord that may lead to numbness, weak arms and legs, poor speech and vision, and tiredness. Michelle Obama's father had multiple sclerosis.

Navy SEALs (NAY-vee SEELZ): A member of the Navy Special Warfare unit, where the "SEAL" stands for "Sea, Air, and Land." Navy SEALs killed Osama bin Laden.

nomination (nah-muh-NAY-shun): If someone receives a nomination, he or she is chosen by a political party to run for an office. Obama won the Democratic nomination for president in 2008.

partisan (PAR-ti-suhn): When a person is partisan, he or she heavily favors and supports a particular party or cause. A partisan voter might vote for a political candidate who is a member of their political party, even if that voter likes a candidate from a different party better.

political science (puh-LIT-uh-kul SYE-euhns): Political science is the study of government and politics. Obama studied political science at Columbia University.

politics (PAWL-uh-tiks): Politics refers to the actions and practices of the government. Obama's first job in politics was as a member of the Illinois state senate.

prejudice (PREJ-uh-dis): Prejudice is having a bad opinion about someone without good reason. As an African American, Obama had to overcome prejudice.

primaries (PRY-mair-eez): Primaries are elections in which members of a political party nominate candidates for office. Obama's main rival during the 2008 presidential primaries was Hillary Rodham Clinton.

recessions (ri-SESH-uns): Recessions are periods of time when the economy slows. The US and world economies were in recessions during President Obama's first term in office.

Republican (ri-PUB-li-kun): A Republican is someone who is a member of the Republican political party. John McCain was a Republican.

scholarship (SKAW-lur-ship): A scholarship is money given to help pay for a student's education. Obama's father received a scholarship to study at the University of Hawaii.

sponsored (SPAWN-surd): If a politician sponsored a bill, he or she proposed it and urged it to be passed. As a senator, Obama sponsored many bills.

THE UNITED STATES GOVERNMENT

The United States government is divided into three equal branches: the executive, the legislative, and the judicial. This division helps prevent abuses of power because each branch has to answer to the other two. No one branch can become too powerful.

EXECUTIVE BRANCH

President
Vice President
Departments

The job of the executive branch is to enforce the laws. It is headed by the president, who serves as the spokesperson for the United States around the world. The president has the power to sign bills into law. He or she also appoints important officials, such as federal judges, who are then confirmed by the US Senate. The president is also the commander in chief of the US military. He or she is assisted by the vice president, who takes over if the president dies or cannot carry out the duties of the office.

The executive branch also includes various departments, each focused on a specific topic. They include the Defense Department, the Justice Department, and the Agriculture Department. The department heads, along with other officials such as the vice president, serve as the president's closest advisers, called the cabinet.

LEGISLATIVE BRANCH

Congress: Senate and the
House of Representatives

The job of the legislative branch is to make the laws. It consists of Congress, which is divided into two parts: the Senate and the House of Representatives. The Senate has 100 members, and the House of Representatives has 435 members. Each state has two senators. The number of representatives a state has varies depending on the state's population.

Besides making laws, Congress also passes budgets and enacts taxes. In addition, it is responsible for declaring war, maintaining the military, and regulating trade with other countries.

JUDICIAL BRANCH

Supreme Court
Courts of Appeals
District Courts

The job of the judicial branch is to interpret the laws. It consists of the nation's federal courts. Trials are held in district courts. During trials, judges must decide what laws mean and how they apply. Courts of appeals review the decisions made in district courts.

The nation's highest court is the Supreme Court. If someone disagrees with a court of appeals ruling, he or she can ask the Supreme Court to review it. The Supreme Court may refuse. The Supreme Court makes sure that decisions and laws do not violate the Constitution.

CHOOSING THE PRESIDENT

It may seem odd, but American voters don't elect the president directly. Instead, the president is chosen using what is called the Electoral College.

Each state gets as many votes in the Electoral College as its combined total of senators and representatives in Congress. For example, Iowa has two senators and four representatives, so it gets six electoral votes. Although the District of Columbia does not have any voting members in Congress, it gets three electoral votes. Usually, the candidate who wins the most votes in any given state receives all of that state's electoral votes.

To become president, a candidate must get more than half of the Electoral College votes. There are a total of 538 votes in the Electoral College, so a candidate needs 270 votes to win. If nobody receives 270 Electoral College votes, the House of Representatives chooses the president.

With the Electoral College system, the person who receives the most votes nationwide does not always receive the most electoral votes. This happened most recently in 2016, when Hillary Clinton received nearly 2.9 million more national votes than Donald J. Trump. Trump became president because he had more Electoral College votes.

The White House is the official home of the president of the United States. It is located at 1600 Pennsylvania Avenue NW in Washington, DC. In 1792, a contest was held to select the architect who would design the president's home. James Hoban won. Construction took eight years.

The first president, George Washington, never lived in the White House. The second president, John Adams, moved into the house in 1800, though the inside was not yet complete. During the War of 1812, British soldiers burned down much of the White House. It was rebuilt several years later.

The White House was changed through the years. Porches were added, and President Theodore Roosevelt added the West Wing. President William Taft changed the shape of the presidential office, making it into the famous Oval Office. While Harry Truman was president, the old house was discovered to be structurally weak. All the walls were reinforced with steel, and the rooms were rebuilt.

Today, the White House has 132 rooms (including 35 bathrooms), 28 fireplaces, and 3 elevators. It takes 570 gallons of paint to cover the outside of the six-story building. The White House provides the president with many ways to relax. It includes a putting green, a jogging track, a swimming pool, a basketball and tennis court, and beautifully landscaped gardens. The White House also has a movie theater, a billiard room, and a one-lane bowling alley.

PRESIDENTIAL PERKS

The job of president of the United States is challenging. It is probably one of the most stressful jobs in the world. Because of this, presidents are paid well, though not nearly as well as the leaders of large corporations. In 2020, the president earned $400,000 a year. Presidents also receive extra benefits that make the demanding job a little more appealing.

★ **Camp David:** In the 1940s, President Franklin D. Roosevelt chose this heavily wooded spot in the mountains of Maryland to be the presidential retreat, where presidents can relax. Even though it is a retreat, world business is conducted there. Most famously, President Jimmy Carter met with Middle Eastern leaders at Camp David in 1978. The result was a peace agreement between Israel and Egypt.

★ *Air Force One:* The president flies on a jet called *Air Force One*. It is a Boeing 747-200B that has been modified to meet the president's needs. *Air Force One* is the size of a large home. It is equipped with a dining room, sleeping quarters, a conference room, and office space. It also has two kitchens that can provide food for up to 100 people.

★ **The Secret Service:** While not the most glamorous of the president's perks, the Secret Service is one of the most important. The Secret Service is a group of highly trained agents who protect the president and the president's family.

★ **The Presidential State Car:** The presidential state car is a customized Cadillac limousine. It has been armored to protect the president in case of attack. Inside the plush car are a foldaway desk, an entertainment center, and a communications console.

★ **The Food:** The White House has five chefs who will make any food the president wants. The White House also has an extensive wine collection and vegetable and fruit gardens.

★ **Retirement:** A former president receives a pension, or retirement pay, of just under $208,000 a year. Former presidents also receive health care coverage and Secret Service protection for the rest of their lives.

QUALIFICATIONS

To run for president, a candidate must
- ★ be at least 35 years old
- ★ be a citizen who was born in the United States
- ★ have lived in the United States for 14 years

TERM OF OFFICE

A president's term of office is four years. No president can stay in office for more than two terms.

ELECTION DATE

The presidential election takes place every four years on the first Tuesday after November 1.

INAUGURATION DATE

Presidents are inaugurated on January 20.

OATH OF OFFICE

I do solemnly swear I will faithfully execute the office of the President of the United States and will to the best of my ability preserve, protect, and defend the Constitution of the United States.

WRITE A LETTER TO THE PRESIDENT

One of the best things about being a US citizen is that Americans get to participate in their government. They can speak out if they feel government leaders aren't doing their jobs. They can also praise leaders who are going the extra mile. Do you have something you'd like the president to do? Should the president worry more about the environment and the effects of climate change? Should the government spend more money on our schools? You can write a letter to the president to say how you feel!

> 1600 Pennsylvania Avenue NW
> Washington, DC 20500

You can even write a message to the president at **whitehouse.gov/contact**.

FOR MORE INFORMATION

BOOKS

MacCarald, Clara. *Michelle Obama: Health Advocate.*
Mankato, MN: The Child's World, 2018.

McDonnell, Julia. *Before Barack Obama Was President.*
New York, NY: Gareth Stevens, 2019.

Small, Cathleen. *Active Citizenship.*
New York, NY: Lucent, 2018.

Torres, John Albert. *How Barack Obama Fought the War
on Terrorism.* New York, NY: Enslow, 2017.

Wilson, Jamia, and Andrea Pippins (illustrator).
Young, Gifted, and Black: Meet 52 Black Heroes from Past and Present.
Minneapolis, MN: Wide Eyed Editions, 2018.

INTERNET SITES

Visit our website for lots of links about
Barack Obama and other US presidents:

childsworld.com/links

*Note to Parents, Teachers, and Librarians: We routinely verify our web links to make
sure they are safe, active sites. Encourage your readers to check them out!*